Writing Sociology Essays

A guide for A-level students

Murray Morison and Jim Pey

Lecturers in Sociology,
South East Essex Sixth Form College, Benfleet

Longman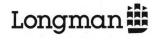

LONGMAN GROUP LIMITED
Longman House, Burnt Mill, Harlow, Essex CM20 2JE, England

First published 1985
Second impression 1987

ISBN 0 582 35490 0

Set in $9\frac{1}{2}$/12pt Ehrhardt Roman, Linotron 202

Printed in Great Britain by Bell and Bain Ltd., Glasgow

British Library Cataloguing in Publication Data

Morison, Murray
   Writing sociology essays: a guide for A-level students.
   1. Social sciences – Authorship
   I. Title   II. Pey, Jim
   808'.0663021   H61.8

Contents

Preface   1

Introduction   2

1 Research and Planning   3

2 Writing Sociology Essays   6

3 Sample Essays   16

4 The Examination   58

Acknowledgements

We are indebted to the Associated Examining Board and the University of Oxford Delegacy of Local Examinations for permission to reproduce past examination questions. The Associated Examining Board wish to state that any answers and hints on answers are the sole responsibility of the authors and have not been provided or approved by the Board. We are also indebted to students Julie Adams, Fran Lemon and Karen Batter for permission to reproduce their essays.

Preface

We have written this book especially for GCE A-level students, although it will be of use to other students following introductory courses in Sociology. In our experience we have found that essay writing, at this level, does not come easily to most students. Our aim is to provide students with useful and flexible techniques for essay writing. It must be clearly stated that this is not a model answer book. In such books (a) the impression is given that there is only one 'right' answer and (b) the method of constructing the essay is not adequately given.

Our approach in this book is to analyse questions in such a way that the student is provided with a basic framework, which can be developed, and around which they can construct a sound answer. The preparation for essays and the problems of revision and examinations have also been dealt with.

We have used recent questions from a number of examination boards, touching on most parts of the A-level syllabus. Limitations of space necessarily meant that not all concepts, research and issues could be explained in detail. However, full indication is given of how answers can be formulated and presented.

To avoid 'cluttering up' the text with excessive footnotes we have not given full references for those authors who are discussed in detail in the main A-level texts.

Introduction

Come the exams, you will not only have to know quite a lot about Sociology, you will also have to be able to write what you know, at speed, under exam conditions. In this book we will show you how to prepare for exams by writing sound essays throughout your course of study. More important, we will indicate how to plan effective essays. Many students fail to do themselves justice through a lack of essay writing skills and examination technique.

While this guide includes a number of specific essays, its purpose is not to provide the 'right answers'. Rather it will show how to prepare for and effectively answer examination questions. To do this we have used two basic techniques. The first is to include essays written under test conditions by students. Generally these essays are of a high standard. We have annotated the essays with comments to highlight the good points and the weaknesses. The second approach we have used is to analyse certain A-level questions, and to try to show in a visual way the relationship between the various arguments suggested by the question. To do this we have used 'thought-webs' or 'mind-maps'. Students have generally found this a very flexible method of setting out ideas, which helps them to structure their arguments in the answer.

We have chosen as wide a range of questions as possible, from a number of different examination boards. While no book of this length could be completely comprehensive, most of the major syllabus areas are covered.

The answers given in this book to questions are just suggestions. There are many ways a question can be answered. What this book seeks to demonstrate are some of the techniques behind the construction of good essays.

Using the book

While doing your coursework, study the questions in the area you are dealing with. When you are set an essay follow the guidelines suggested in the next two sections on research and writing essays. Practice making detailed plans before you start writing. Through this practice, your ability to write a well argued essay will improve. We would recommend the 'thought-web' approach to planning, as this enables you to have an overview of the different arguments and ideas you will be presenting.

Study the full-length essays that have been included, to see the way in which they have structured their ideas and linked them to the question. Try to incorporate any good points of technique in your own essays.

When the exam approaches, the book can be used partly for revision, and also you can use the questions provided to practice exam-length essays, which can be checked back against the detailed plans provided.

Note: no references are given for studies that are easily found in the main text books currently available.

Research and planning

Your success in the A-level examination will depend on how effectively you answer the questions that are set. Your ability to do this will depend on how well you have prepared yourself over the year or two years of your course. Coursework essays that have been efficiently researched and imaginatively written will deepen your sociological understanding and provide good material to revise from.

Research

If you are preparing for a specific essay title, then make sure that you understand something of the implications of that title before starting your research. You need to 'de-code' the question sufficiently to make sure that your research is on the right lines. A question on organisations, for example, might usefully cover more than just bureaucracies, and you could follow up issues relating to scientific management, total institutions, formal and informal organisations and so on. It would depend on how the question was worded. When the 'field' of your research is clearer, then start collecting material for the essay.

Use of texts
There are a considerable number of texts you may have access to. Make good use of the table of contents and the index to find the relevant pages for the points you wish to follow up. Skim through unfamiliar material, firstly to get an overview of what is being said, and secondly to locate parts that are of particular relevance to your needs. Make brief notes in your own words, ensuring that the important details (names, dates, statistics) are correct. Avoid the temptation to write the essay straight from the textbook.

Use of other books
Specific points or illustrative material will be available in library books. Here particular care must be taken not to get lost in detail, but to focus on studies or arguments directly related to the essay in hand. Again the index and chapter headings will prove vital signposts. Going beyond the textbook in this way is an important preparation for the eventual exam.

Other sources
Certain newspapers, particularly *The Guardian*, and journals like *New Society*, often have articles that are up to date and are of value for particular parts of your course. You can also make use of TV documentaries, tape recordings, and even novels where appropriate. Such sources allow you to apply the sociological perspective to current social situations. Reference books like *Social Trends* contain much useful statistical material.

Research and Planning

Note taking

Your notes should be clear, with sufficient detail, but not over long. Record the main points of an argument, with sufficient illustrative material to back it up, but without getting lost in the finer points. Set your notes out neatly, because although you will be writing an essay based on them, they can also be used later for revision. Make liberal use of headings, sub-headings, underlining and colour. This will make your notes clearer to follow and more interesting to read.

Cards

Many students find that summaries of key studies put on file cards can prove to be very useful. This can be done while preparing coursework material, and can be invaluable for revision purposes later. Material on cards can be more easily sorted out and manipulated when you come to plan your essay.

Planning

Essays packed with good material, but presented haphazardly, will never gain very much credit. While planning an essay, particularly early on in the course, may not seem very easy, it will serve to clarify the ideas that are being written about. The plan should reflect the broad outline of the argument being presented. Before a plan can be made for a given question, the question needs to be analysed. To accomplish this, underline the key words in the question or title. Then try to restate in your own words what the question is saying. Scribble down, in any order, the points that you might cover in your answer. These can be worked later into a structured plan. Note whether the question is asking you to 'discuss' or 'explain' or 'evaluate' or 'compare', and whether you are expected to 'be critical' or to 'give examples'.

Although it may seem like stating the obvious, a good essay will have a beginning, a middle and an end. We suggest two basic ways you might structure your answer.

1 The 'evaluation'
   Introduction, with main terms defined
   Development of ideas, with illustrations and criticisms
   Conclusion, in relation to question set
2 The 'debate'
   Introduction with main issues outlined
   One line of argument (with theory and evidence)
   The opposing line of argument (with theory and evidence)
   Discussion and conclusion

While the overall plan will probably conform to one of these patterns, the detailed structure of the arguments may be considerably more complex. The use of 'thought-webs' or 'mind-maps' can be most helpful in allowing you to build up your plan around certain ideas. This technique is illustrated in the next section. The finished plan for a cousework essay should show where the main arguments and ideas are to be introduced, and what theorists and studies are to be mentioned at various points. Even under examination conditions a brief plan can prove invaluable, and can help ensure that the essay has a good structure.

Writing Sociology Essays

Both the examination and cousework essays are used to elicit from you your ability to describe and to analyse the relationship between sociological theory and specific examples of sociological research; to give a coherent account of a topic; to select and weigh evidence in support of an argument; to diagnose and suggest solutions to problems; to express critical judgements; and to make comparisons.

The lack of success at A-level is often the result of either:

a the 'Sunday Supplement style': an account that lacks detailed support and argument and is written 'off the top of one's head'; or

b O-level effect: here students fail to bridge the gap between the O-level essay (which is more factually based), and the A-level essay (with greater emphasis on the relationship between theory and actual research).

The highest grades are achieved by those who are able to present, in an orderly and coherent way, a mass of information relating to a topic, and to critically analyse it. Often a major weakness of essays done at home, or under test conditions, is irrelevance. You must answer the question as it is set. Make a plan. Then when your plan is complete check that it does really answer the specific question. When writing, make sure that the points made, and the arguments presented, are clearly linked back to the main issues in the question.

The coursework essay

The purpose of this type of essay is to allow you to re-express in your own words, the ideas and arguments relating to a particular issue or question. It is only through re-working the sociological material covered in your course, or gained through research, that you can come to really understand the theories and the studies and their implications. The ability to present complex arguments clearly is a valuable skill. Writing essays can help develop this skill, if you keep in mind certain principles:

1 You should prepare for the essay sufficiently. Do not let every essay be a 'last-minute job', accomplished among the debris of a coffee-bar, or while keeping half an eye on the TV.

2 Make a detailed plan. Know where you are going to present different arguments and ideas before you start. The plan provides you with an overview of what you are going to write at all stages, and this can improve the way you present the ideas at any particular point, because you can relate them to what is to come.

3 Make your beginning relevant. Take some key aspect of the question as your launching-point, perhaps indicating the general angle or approach that you are going to follow.

4 Link the main stages of your argument. Give signposts that the reader can follow.

5 Generally allow each new idea or study a paragraph of its own, but link the paragraphs one to another, so that the argument flows.

6 Finally, make sure that when you draw towards the end, you round off what you are saying. Establish a conclusion, or at least sum up what you see as being the balance of the arguments you have presented. The conclusion provides you with an opportunity to critically overview the arguments you have presented.

The coursework essay should be comprehensive in its coverage of a topic, both as an aid to understanding the issues and because it will be useful for revision purposes later. It needs therefore to be accurate in the details that you quote. Make an effort to explain the ideas and theories as far as you are able. Often the essay will be the final piece of work that you do on a topic before preparing for the exam, and it is at this point that you should put in the time and effort to ensure you really understand what you are writing about.

The examination essay

The purpose of an examination essay is to test your knowledge of sociology, your understanding of its theories and your skill at giving expression to both of these things. Your purpose with the essay is to score high marks. This you will do by showing that you really comprehend the question, and then by providing a well-organised and informed answer. This whole book is designed to help you to develop the techniques to accomplish this, but some preliminary pointers will help.

Always read the question through at least twice to make sure that you grasp what it is actually asking. The folly of answering a question that has not been set is obvious, and results in much wasted effort. Then go through the question again and underline the key terms. This will ensure that you do not miss any vital points. Then make a plan. It does not have to be elaborate, as under test conditions you will not have much time. Still it is surprising how much you can put down on paper in a couple of minutes, and this will be time well spent. When completed, do check that your plan does in fact answer the actual question.

We suggest that there are three elements to bear in mind while you write an examination essay: structure, content and style. The *structure* of the essay refers to the way you organise the argument. It should be logical, clear and appropriate. You must avoid giving a succession of unrelated points. Your argument should unfold through linked papragraphs, and the main sections of the essay should form a coherent whole. The *content* refers to the substance of the essay, which must be appropriate and in sufficient detail.

Writing Sociology Essays

The *style* is your own way of expressing the ideas. The essay should be as clear as possible, but there is room for a little ingenuity and individuality in presentation.

We will first consider a worked example, and then how to develop 'mind maps'.

'Schools do not merely react to children with varying qualities and capacities in a neutral way: they play an active part in creating children who are more or less educable, more or less knowledgeable, more or less manageable.'

(Bilton *et al.: Introductory Sociology*) Explain and discuss.

(AEB June 1983)

Analysis of the question

The first step is to go through the question looking for the key words and phrases. These can be underlined for greater clarity:

'<u>Schools</u> do not merely react to children with varying qualities and capacities in a <u>neutral</u> way: they play an <u>active</u> part in <u>creating</u> <u>children</u> who are more or less <u>educable</u>, more or less <u>knowledgeable</u>, more or less <u>manageable</u>.' <u>Explain</u> and <u>discuss</u>.

The question can now be considered in more detail. The central focus is on the <u>school</u>. What is meant by the school being <u>active</u> rather than <u>neutral</u> in 'creating children'? It is the <u>role of the school</u> (rather than the home – or the class system) in influencing the child's <u>ability to learn</u> (educability), regulating the child's <u>access to knowledge</u> (knowledgeability), and <u>maintaining control</u> (manageability), that is sought. It is necessary to make sure the answer both <u>explains</u> these concepts, and illustrates them. In addition a critical <u>discussion</u> or assessment is required.

Planning the question

When preparing an essay for class a full plan is a very helpful aid. Under test or exam conditions a brief plan is still very important. The plan can ensure that the content is adequate, and related to the question, and that the line of argument is appropriate.

As a start, a list of points or studies you might include, can be made. Write them as they occur to you, and worry about organisation later. At this stage, go for completeness.

Studies of schools	Historical viewpoint	Other types of explanation
Jackson and Marsden	Pre-war	Home background
Rosenthal and Jacobson	Tripartite system	and cultural
Rist	Comprehensives	deprivation
Hargreaves	Public schools	IQ and heredity
Lacey		Class, ideology
Willis		and exploitation
Keddie		
Ford		
Ball		
Rutter		
Bowles and Gintis		

While this is not an exhaustive list of all that might be relevant to the question, there is more than enough to be dealt with in one essay. When there is time (when writing an essay at home for example) then approaching it this way will enable you to to see the broader context within which the question lies. You are now ready to move onto a specific essay plan. This can be in the form of a 'mind-map' or in a sequential form. We will illustrate both here. Under exam conditions briefer plans would be all you will have time for.

In making your plan, what you are trying to do is set up the framework of an argument, that actually answers the question set. A clear plan will be a great aid in producing a well-formulated essay.

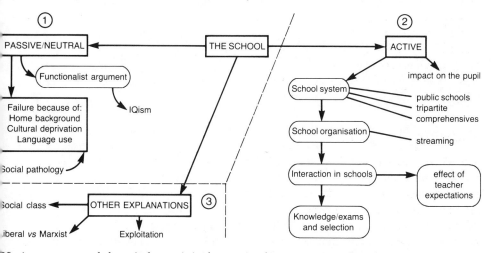

Having constructed the mind-map it is then a simple matter to number the various parts of it in the order which you want to write about them. The essay can then be started. An alternative preparation is to do a straightforward plan. Use whichever method suits you best.

Writing Sociology Essays

School as passive
Functionalist argument; IQ and heredity
Social pathology/cultural deprivation; home background; language

Schools as active
Active in enabling the child to learn (or not)
Active in defining what counts as knowledge
Active in sorting, selecting and controlling children

How do schools influence children?
Schools systems: public schools and finance; tripartite *vs* comprehensive (Halsey, Ball, Rutter etc.)
Organisation of schooling: streaming (Hargreaves, Lacey etc.); mixed ability; fragmentation (Bowles and Gintis); schools do differ (Rutter); learning to labour (Willis)

Interaction in schools
Teacher expectations; self-fulfilling prophesy (Rosenthal and Jacobson etc)

Knowledge
Academic vs everyday; classification and framing (Young; Bernstein).

Other explanations
Class analysis (Bourdieu *etc*); and conclusion (e.g. Solihull)

What follows is a suggested answer to the question that we have been analysing. The essay is set out on the left, and on the right there are comments on why this particular approach has been taken. It is worth noting of course that there is no one 'right' answer, and quite a different but equally valid approach could be taken.

To consider that schools merely react in a neutral way, is to see them as being 'fair' and largely apolitical. **(1)** While bemoaning the bias of certain teachers or subjects, the conservative view of education stresses it is fair. The functionalist approach also sees the system on the whole as providing equal opportunity, and sorting people out according to their inherent talents. The argument behind the 11+, for example, rested on the idea that it was a dispassionate system of sorting children according to their innate ability.

Although critical of the functionalist approach, those writers like Douglas and Plowden, who stressed the impact of home conditions and the idea of cultural deprivation, to a considerable degree shifted attention away from the processes occuring in schools.

(1) The introduction avoids being too general, and takes up an aspect of the question straight away.

To see the schools as playing an active part, is to concentrate on the way in which participants in the school interact, and the way schools process students. **(2)** The wider context is not ignored, but the spotlight shifts to the arena of the classroom itself. In this arena students are labelled, differentiated, given or denied access to certain types of knowledge and examinations. They may learn, learn to fail, or learn to labour. **(3)** Teachers are seen, from this point of view as an extension of general societal processes of selection and control. Doubts about the 'fairness' of the school system can be seen when considering changes this century. **(4)**

The old elementary – grammar school division in the state sector was considered to favour the well-to-do, and was replaced by the tripartite system as a result of Butler's 1944 Education Act. The 11+ 'sorting system' was meant to give an equal chance to children of all classes, to enter schools that would suit their abilities – the schools having 'parity of esteem'. Recent work by Halsey demonstrates that the tripartite system did mean that many more could go to grammar schools, but they tended to be disproportionately middle class. The tax subsidies to the public schools, and their higher pupil-teacher ratios, have ensured that for those who can afford them advantages could still be bought.

In the last 20 years the tripartite system has been mostly replaced by comprehensives. The classic study by Ford, and the more recent account by Ball **(5)** show how to some extent the basic inequalities of the tripartite system have persisted in the new arrangements.

Rutter, in his book '15,000 Hours', argues that different comprehensive schools can produce widely differing results and are far from 'neutral'. The attitude of staff, and the nature of the organisation of the schools, seemed to be of particular importance. The causes of these differences are illustrated by earlier work on the effects of streaming. **(6)** Both the study of a secondary modern by Hargeaves and of a grammar school in Manchester by Lacey, showed how streaming affected attitudes towards school. The lower streams in the secondary modern tended to become 'delinquescent'. Similarly, Lacey found that students were differentiated, and tended to polarise along class lines. The lower streams received mainly working class pupils, who often became disruptive. In both these cases the organisation of the school was active in producing effects on students – often of an unintended kind.

The marxist writers Bowles and Gintis see schools as active in a different sense. For them the schools serve as part of the capitalist system. The very way in which knowledge is divided up into subjects and lessons, means that the experience of education is fragmented.

(2) Some of the terms used in the title are being defined here. It is good if definitions can be woven into the early part of an essay.

(3) There may not be room to discuss Willis' research in the essay, but using this phrase at least shows familiarity with it.

(4) This introduces the next section, which will take a developmental/historical perspective.

(5) Essays should not be lists of names, but it is necessary to mention certain key studies, and to relate ideas to research.

(6) This makes a (slightly artificial) link between Rutter's work and that of Hargreaves and Lacey a decade earlier. It is a point of good style to try and connect together the various points you make in an essay.

11

Writing Sociology Essays

Just as with the similar fragmentation in working life, the individual does not come to understand how the system is being exploitative.

The impact of schools has also been illustrated by the influential work of Rosenthal and Jacobson with their idea of the self-fulfilling prophecy. Their research suggested that teacher expectations had a definite effect on the performance of students. While their methodology has been criticised, **(7)** other research supports their general theory. Rist, observing one classroom teacher, noted how the very way she had arranged her pupils' seating, and the position of the blackboard, tended to work in favour of those she saw as brighter (usually middle-class pupils) and against those she considered dull (usually working-class). The work of Keddie comes to similar conclusions; she found students in different streams were given access to different types of knowledge.

(7) In an essay on labelling theory as such, you could go into this in more detail; here it is enough to acknowledge that their work did not 'prove' the idea of the self-fulfilling prophecy.

Michael Young argues along the same lines, with his idea of the division of knowledge in schools into the academic, literate and individual, as compared to the non-academic/everyday, oral and group-related. Children in schools, he says, do not all have the same chance of acquiring different types of knowledge, and it is the academic, non-everyday knowledge that is the most rewarded. This is the sort of knowledge that is often part of the middle-classes' 'cultural capital'.

Recent research has shown beyond any doubt that schools are active in their 'creating children' with different abilities. To conclude from this that the analysis must stop at the school gates would be incorrect. The wider social context within which schooling takes place must be considered, especially the role of social class. Schooling as a whole is seen as exploitative, and as part of the capitalist 'state ideological apparatus' by marxists like Althusser. Marxists, or indeed 'liberals' like Halsey, would argue for the need to see education in a broader political framework. **(8)** Nevertheless it would appear that the activity within the school must also be closely studied.

(8) The conclusion here enables the argument about schools to be set in a broader context.

It must be stressed that the essay above is only one way in which the question could have been answered. A conscious effort was made to deal with each of the points raised in the question, but fewer studies could have been dealt with, though looked at in more detail. The important thing is that a clear line of argument is given, that is broadly linked to the actual question set.

'What happens to us at work, the demands the job makes on our energy, skills and temper, the relationships we develop with colleagues

or our employers behaviour towards us have profound effects on us which carry over into other areas of our life.' (Noble: *Modern Britain: Structure and Change*)
Examine the sociological evidence for this statement.

(AEB November 1981)

At first sight this might appear to be a 'work and leisure' question, but it is more than this. Various aspects of work are touched on, and 'other areas of our life' can be interpreted quite broadly. To show how a 'web of ideas' might be constructed for such a question we will divide it into two parts. The initial main points we put down will reflect the key parts of the question.

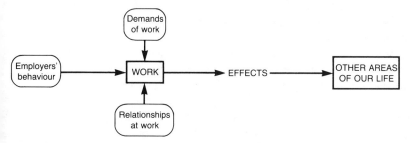

This picks out some of the main aspects of the quote, and we can use it as a framework to which we can attach further ideas and studies. The idea of 'sociological evidence' has not been included yet, and the 'other areas' remain undefined. Before we can tackle the question we should decide how many areas it will be appropriate to write about. We should also be thinking of what empirical studies or theoretical perspectives it will be necessary to introduce, even though we will not deal with all in equal depth.

Our more elaborated 'web' or 'map' could look like this:

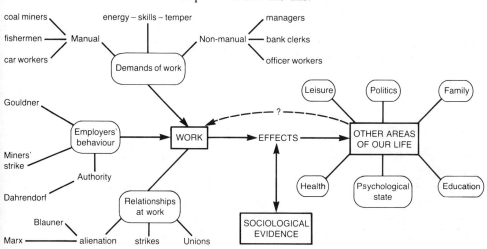

13

Writing Sociology Essays

This would be quite adequate to use as the basis of an essay. The diagram could be made fuller and more detailed if it was for a home-based essay, or for revision purposes. The studies associated with the 'other areas of our life' have not been filled in, but even under exam conditions it might help to scribble some down – e.g. leisure (Parker, McIntosh); politics (Goldthorpe and Lockwood, instrumentalism); family (Seeley, Gans, Tunstall, Klein); education (Douglas, Lacey); health (Townsend, Doyle); psychological state/alienation (Gallie, Mallet, Blauner).

It can be helpful to use another colour to connect different parts of the 'web'. Even without doing this it is now possible to write the essay always having a complete overview in front of you. The order in which you are going to take the ideas can then be numbered. If other points occur to you, they can be added, e.g. the effect of other areas of life on work is illustrated by Goldthorpe and Lockwood's *Affluent Worker*.

Has the emergence of pressure groups transformed the nature of power in western industrial societies?   (Cambridge June 1983)

The question initially requires a consideration of the nature of power through an historical perspective which traces the emergence of pressure groups and representative democracy in western industrial society. The central argument then becomes, does power remain in the hands of the few, i.e. the ruling class or elite, or has it dispersed with the development of pressure groups within the context of representative democracy?

The central concern is the nature of power. The key issues, theories and evidence can be clearly and simply depicted as follows:

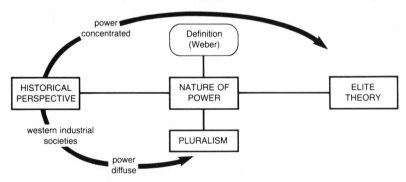

With a clear outline we can now proceed to develop the different aspects of the argument.

Referring to Weber a brief distinction can be made between power and authority. Using the UK, USA, France and Germany as examples a brief, descriptive account of the changing nature of power in western industrial societies can be made. Both marxism and elite theory (Pareto and Mosca)

14

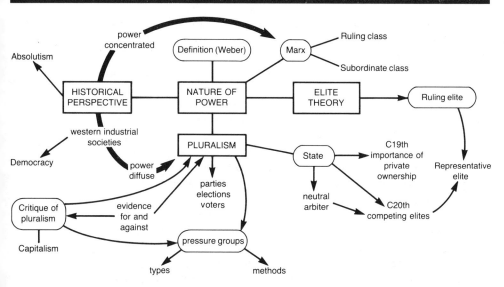

suggest in different ways that a relatively small group dominates a relatively large subordinate group. The pluralist model (Dahl, Reisman) suggests that in western industrial democracies power has become increasingly dispersed through the electoral and pressure group systems. The state acts as a neutral arbiter of competing interests, no one dominating. The continued presence of elites is justified inasmuch as they are representative of membership (e.g. TUC Trade Unions and CBI). The pluralist model can be criticised on its own terms, that the position, size and material resources will influence in an unequal way the amount and quality of access a group has to the resources of the state. It is also easier for some to form pressure groups than for others, e.g. the old, disabled, etc. Empirical evidence supporting this model is accused of being influenced and directed by the model itself (for: Dahl and Hewitt; against: Bachrach and Baratz; Lukes; Mills; Saunders).

However, the central critique highlights how the pluralists appear to ignore the socio-economic context within which the liberal democratic process takes place, i.e. capitalism. The assumptions of consensus and competition which underpin the pluralist model tend to ignore the fundamentally unequal nature of capitalist society which, it could be argued, operates on just the opposite assumptions, i.e. conflict and unfair competition. This is the essence of the marxist critique and, according to them, the dominant interests of capital are never seriously threatened (Miliband; Westergaard and Resler; Poulantzas). Weberians would further point to the unaccountable and essentially undemocratic organisational bureaucracy, both state and private, as the central feature of western industrial societies.

In the light of the evidence and argument does the pluralist model hold and if not, which alternative perspective or combination of perspectives is most adequate?

Sample Essays

'The affluence of many workers in industry and the growth of White collar workers and their unionisation, is leading to a convergence of the upper working-class and lower middleclass.' Is it?

Many people have suggested that the affluence of many workers in industry and the growth of white-collar work and its unionisation has led to a convergence between the upper working-class and lower middle-class. This idea links in with the ideas of embourgeoisement and proletarianisation which were part of the whole line of thinking in the 1960s. At the time, nobody questioned it, but now, questions are beginning to be raised. **(1)**

In fact, many studies have been done in this area. One such study was the 'The affluent worker in the class structure', by Lockwood and Goldthorpe. **(2)** In this study, the authors chose a prosperous area with a number of new industries which paid workers highly. **(3)** The area was also one to which many people had migrated. Therefore, the chances of embourgeoisement occurring here were very high. If workers, in this area were not moving into the middle class, then it would be fair to say that the process of embourgoisement was a myth. **(4)** Lockwood and Goldthorpe chose three main areas in which to question these affluent workers: economic, normative and relational. They said that if it was found that the 229 manual workers in their sample compared to the 54 white-collar workers they had chosen, then embourgeoisement was taking place. **(5)**

Under the economic heading, it was found that many of the manual workers had higher wages or comparable wages to most white-collar workers. However, this was through overtime, usually, and the average manual worker worked a forty-to-fifty-hour week which interfered with home life, whilst the white-collar workers were 'better-off' in all respects. They had fringe benefits and perks and gained intrinsic satisfaction from their work. The manual workers, though, saw work as a place purely to earn money, in extrinsic terms. They gained no satisfaction from it at all. However, similarities in the economic aspect were found in that both groups had a family-centred, privatised life. Lockwood and Goldthorpe said that this was due to increased economic consumption on the part of manual workers which meant that their homes were more comfortable and modern. Also, although white-collar workers did not see their jobs in purely extrinsic terms, many were joining unions because they helped in the pursuit of money. This instrumental collectivism was found to be another aspect of convergence, although the attitude of the white-collar workers to unions was

(1) Effective statement of main issues makes good, brief introduction.

(2) date (1968) would help.

(3) i.e. Luton.

(4) This makes the important point that the Luton study was a 'critical case'.

(5) Grammatically, this sentence is a bit suspect, but it does state the argument and efficiently introduces illustrative data.

slightly different from the manual workers in that they did not identify with the trade union movement and saw themselves as set apart from the type of unions that the manual workers belonged to.

Under the other headings of normative and relational **(6)** Lockwood and Goldthorpe found no convergence. It was true that the manual workers had a more privatised life, but this was due to economic factors, as was their support for trade unions. On the whole, these workers still supported the Labour Party (80% voted Labour in 1959, more than for the working class alone), **(7)** although purely for instrumental terms and not the reasons of traditional working-class solidarity. In relationships also, there was or appeared to be no convergence. The workers still had kin and neighbours and fairly informal meetings. The white-collar workers, though, tended to rely more on friends at work and individuals who were neither neighbours nor kin. These findings also were found by Stephen Hill, who made a study of dockers. **(8)** So it appears that if any convergence has taken place, of the working class becoming middle-class, it is slight and rests purely on economic factors. Lockwood and Goldthorpe made this conclusion and said that convergence in some spheres, but not embourgeoisement, was occuring.

The same findings also apply to proletarianisation; when the middle class become working class. C. W. Mills in 'White Collar' and Lockwood in 'The Blackcoated Worker' are two sociologists who have studied this 'process'. Both suggested that the growth of the white-collar sector (in 1851, clerks were 1% of labour force, in the 1970s an 14%) **(9)** have led to a decrease in status for these workers. Some have also suggested that increased literacy and numeracy have increased in the number of potential clerks and 'de-skilled' their position. C. W. Mills argues that 'status panic' then follows and in trying to keep their status, conspicuous consumption occurs amongst this group. Therefore, in order to conspicuously consume, more money is needed. In pursuit of this, unionisation occurs.

However, the unions of these people differ from the traditional working-class union and the average white-collar worker does not identify with the working-class. He works away from the factory floor and works more closely with management so he does not identify with working-class people or working-class institutions. Marxists would class this false class consciousness because in their terms, clerks are clearly proletariat because they are property-less. Lockwood, though, rejects this. **(10)** He says that it is not false class consciousness because it reflects a real difference between the position of these people in comparison to the position of manual workers.

(6) Terms 'normative' and relational need brief definition.

(7) point in argument usefully backed up with specific data.

(8) Could add that dockers are 'traditional working class'.

(9) useful illustration.

(10) Lockwood's analysis in terms of 'market situation', 'work situation' and 'status aspiration' should be mentioned.

Sample Essays

C. W. Mills and Ralf Dahrendorf both see the position of the white-collar worker as due to his authority. In Dahrendorf's view of society, class is dependent on authority patterns, and there are those who give orders and those who obey. The white collar worker is in a position of being employed by 'the owners' – the real bourgeoisie – to do work that needs to be done, and in doing so these white-collar workers, although subordinate to their masters, are in a position to give order to others. Thus, Mills and Dahrendorf see these people as being a part of a different class. **(11)** They could be called the petit-bourgeoisie and fitted into a category with people such as teachers and shopkeepers. Mills was not sure what was going to happen to these people, whether they were going to become a new individual middle class, a buffer, or be ground down into the proletariat. Therefore, it appears that there has not really been a convergence between the upper working and lower middle levels of society. Attitudes and values, two things that can mark out strongly what class a person belongs to, are different. Also, the majority of white collar workers see themselves as middle class today although in the fifties, the majority identified with working class. The efficient workers also see themselves as working class and self-assessment of class is important. If someone believes strongly that they belong to a particular class then they may be accepted by other members and acceptance is all-important. The only real convergence in truth has been in economic terms.

(11) Mills calls them 'the New Middle Class'.

Essay by Karen Batter

Structure

The answer is tackled, after a concise introduction, in two parts, embourgeoisement and proletarianisation. This is quite legitimate, as the question obliquely refers to both these issues. A stronger definition of the convergence itself is required early in the essay, mentioning instrumentalism, privatisation and consumerism. The conclusion rounds off the essay quite well, but could return more strongly to theory.

Content

The illustrations used back up the arguments, though specific examples of unionisation could be mentioned, e.g. ASTMS, and the civil service unions. While false class consciousness is discussed, the disagreement between the conflict and interpretive or social action approaches with regard to this could be highlighted in the conclusion. Other useful research includes Weir, and Davis; for a marxist critique of 'instrumentalism' use Westergaard and Resler.

18

The work of Braverman is very important to the proletarianisation issue. Recent work by Roberts on the 'fragmented' class structure could also be used here.

Style

The essay efficiently conveys a lot of information. This business-like approach is helpful, as it is free of 'waffle'.

'Poverty, which used to be studied as a 'social problem', is increasingly being studied as an aspect of structured social inequality'. Describe this change of approach and explain its significance for our understanding of poverty. (AEB November 1981)

The structure of this question, in mentioning the idea of 'social problem' and contrasting it with 'structured social inequality', suggests the steps in which it could be answered. The reasons for the move from one viewpoint to the other would also need to be given. This can be summarised in a 'mind-map'.

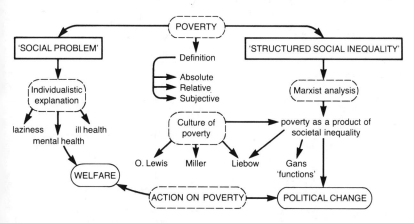

The change in the approach to poverty has come, in part, as a result of the impact of studies such as those of Townsend, Kincaid and Field. They demonstrated that poverty is more widespread than had been generally acknowledged. Coates and Silburn's study of St Anne's in Nottingham show how the poor belong to a fragmented community; Miliband demonstrates their powerlessness. Seeing the poor as a product of the operations of an unequal society has considerable policy implications. A structural explanation would suggest that only structural/political change will finally cope with the problem.

Note that the 'culture of poverty' idea can be seen both as 'individualistic' or as a result of a capitalist cash economy in the Third World. Hence it forms a link between the two types of explanation being considered.

Sample Essays

(a) What do sociologists understand by the word 'underclass'?

                                                      (12 marks)

(b) To what extent is there an ethnically differentiated 'underclass' in Britain?

                                                      (13 marks)

                                                      (AEB June 1981)

A question set in two parts like this is best answered in two separate sections, the length of each depending on the marks allocated. The answer must demonstrate that the term 'underclass' is controversial, as it implies a basic division among the working class. Even when the 'bottom' group is racially distinct, some would argue that they are not really an 'underclass'.

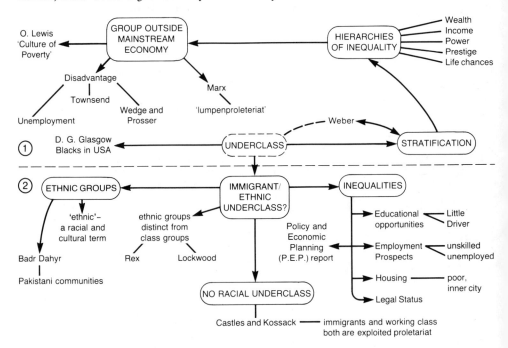

Part (a) is relatively straightforward as it involves defining and illustrating the term 'underclass', which derives in part from the marxian idea of *lumpen-proletariat* and the Weberian idea of a group separated by culture, belief and status from dominant groups in the society. D. Glasgow's work forms a good link between the two parts of the question, as he uses the term 'underclass' to describe blacks in the USA. In part (b) after defining the term 'ethnic', and possibly illustrating it with the idea of a Pakistani ethnic community (Badr Dahyr), Rex and Lockwood's ideas can be considered. Both separately argue that race cannot be analysed in purely class terms. Rex sees ethnic groups in the U.K. as an underclass. The degree to which Pakistanis and

West Indians are 'outside' the system can be illustrated by considering education, employment, housing, legal status, etc. Castles and Kossack reject the idea of an underclass, as they argue that immigrants and the working class are both exploited and are part of the proletariat. This question of objective and subjective class position in society could form the basis of the conclusion.

Explain and discuss the argument that youth represents a class or stratum with interests of its own in opposition to those of adults.

(AEB June 1980)

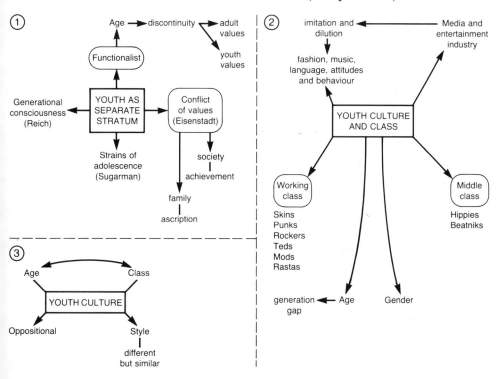

The analysis of youth as a separate stratum forms the starting point for looking at the functionalist perspective in terms of age and 'generational consciousness' (Reich). Alternative viewpoints focus on the mediating influence of social class on youth sub-cultural behaviour, drawing a distinction between working-class youth (e.g. skins) and middle-class youth (e.g. hippies). Other, less class-specific factors also influence the behaviour of youth, e.g. gender and ethnicity.

    The differentiation of adult society is reflected in that of their children, though the media, in popularising peculiarly class-based aspects of youth culture, dilute class differences. The education system perpetuates the division of adult society into that of youth, with the relative success of middle-class youth and the failure of working class youth. Both 'success' and 'failure' can reflect conformist behaviour, and the resistance of many youth sub-cultural groups to 'adult' society can be exaggerated (e.g. mods and rockers).

Any conclusion must take account of the physical, psychological and social changes that are peculiar to adolescence but at the same time recognise that the behaviour and attitudes of youth are mediated by the powerful influence of social class. A variety of youth groups exhibit differences of style in such areas as fashion, language, music, behaviour and attitudes, but these could hardly be described as characteristic of all people or as 'oppositional' to 'adult society' (NCB and NOP surveys). Differences are often exaggerated, becoming 'moral panics', whilst the hippie counter-culture was (a) short-lived and (b) the experiment of a privileged few.

Striking represents one form of industrial action. What other forms are there and how can the varied levels of conflict in different industries be explained? (AEB June 1980)

The question can be clearly divided into four main parts which include:
1 A definition of strikes and the form they take;
2 Other forms of industrial action;
3 Varied levels of conflict in different industries;
4 Explanations of such varied levels.

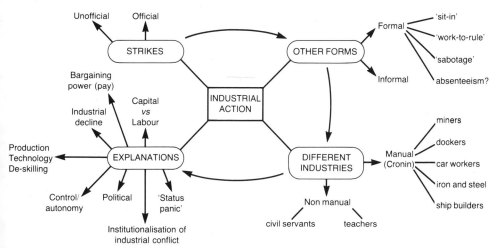

Briefly define what a strike and related actions mean and indicate their frequency. Other forms of industrial action can then be mentioned, with illustrations. Evidence of the varied levels of conflict in different industries requires description before explanation can be given. Cronin is drawn on heavily here with specific reference to manual work, but the increasing industrial action of 'white collar' workers should be highlighted. The explanations given can be supported by using:
1 the classic sociological studies, e.g. Gouldner, Lane and Roberts, etc.,
2 Recent examples, e.g. the print-workers dispute 1983, the miners' strike 1984, the teachers' strike and work-to-rule 1984.
3 More general theoretical explanations, e.g. the marxist and conflict perspectives.

Explanations offer, either implicitly or explicitly, possible solutions – e.g. for marxists a move to the common ownership of the means of production through revolutionary action – whilst others proffer piecemeal change in the attempt to create 'industrial democracy'; others still hold that the fundamental relationship between employer and employee in capitalist society is inevitable and is ultimately in the interests of both groups.

Sample Essays

Organisations have been seen as a threat to individual liberty, and essential for democracy. What light do sociologists throw on this debate?

The term organisation is a fundamental one in sociology, implying a structured set of relationships and the formation and sustaining of groups to achieve specific purposes. This question enables discussion of a key sociological issue, namely the degree to which organisations, arguably essential for democracy to work, actually tend to become anti-democratic. Also implied is the debate about what D. Wrong has called the 'over-socialised view of man'. Do the pressures of socialisation and conformity lead to the individual having no freedom of action?

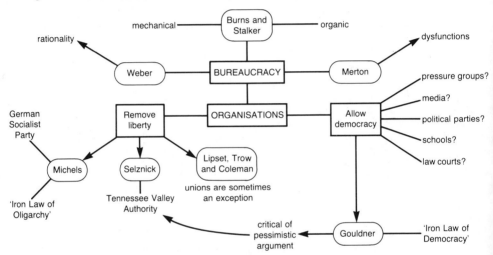

In defining formal organisations, reference to 'bureaucracy' could be made. The rational organisation that underlies bureaucracy, Weber argued, although efficient, would impede individual liberty. Merton questions the efficiency of rule-dominated bureaucracies, a point taken up by Burns and Stalker in their description of organic organisations in contrast to mechanical.

The argument that organisations allow democracy can be illustrated in a number of ways. Political parties and unions are clearly organisations. So are law courts, schools, pressure groups and the media. Each can be said to aid democracy, and also, from the marxist viewpoint, to prevent true freedom. The classic studies of Michels and Selznick argue pessimistically against democracy. In their study of unions, with the exception of the printer's union, Lipset *et al.* tend to agree. Gouldner, quoting Lovejoy's discussions of the 'metaphysical pathos of pessimism' (Worsley, *Problems of Modern Society* 1978) maintains a more optimistic position can be taken, and that democracy also tends to be inevitable in organisations.

'**Changes in the divorce rate since 1900 have resulted from changes in legislation, not from changes in attitudes to marriage**'. **Discuss.**

(Oxford May 1981)

The focus of the essay revolves around two key positions: the one that attributes changes in the divorce rate (DR) to changes in legislation, and the other that sees it in terms of changing attitudes to marriage which leads to legal change, which leads in turn to changes in the DR.

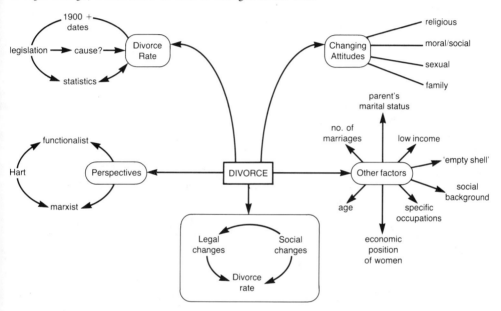

The link between legal changes and an increasing DR should be expressed statistically, indicating the latter as the result of the former. The position that legal changes have emerged and been taken advantage of because of changing attitudes towards marriage and 'other factors' should be comprehensively covered. Key theoretical explanations can be developed making good use of Hart. For the functionalists a high DR is attributable to the changing norms and values of industrial society. An increasingly high value placed on marriage, isolated nuclear family (strain) and increased opportunities to escape from marriage leads to a rising DR. For marxists, marital breakdown can be seen as the result of conflict between (a) the economic demands of capitalism and (b) the normative expectations of the housewife/mother. In summary, then, a legal change *in itself* does not increase the DR, for if all were happily married then the DR would not increase. Rather, it provides the opportunity to resolve pre-existing problems of marital instability which formerly manifested itself in such forms as empty shell marriages and separation.

Sample Essays

'To classify working-class marital relationships as segregated and middle-class ones as joint is an over-simplification.' Discuss. (AEB June 1983)

'March of progress' theorists argue that modern industrialisation has led to the rise of the egalitarian family. Willmott and Young back this up. They argue that there are three stages to the family. Stage 1 is the preindustrial family which is a unit of production. Stage 2 started with the industrial revolution. Here the family was no longer a unit of production, since people now worked for wages. Stage 3 is where Willmott and Young argue that the symmetrical family has developed. Here the nuclear family is not connected closely to the extended family. It is very home-centred. Women also go out to work and they share domestic work with their husbands. Better standards of living, especially for the middle class, have led to the emergence of the 'symmetrical family'. Here husbands and wives spend more time in the home together. Due to the decline of the extended family, the couple share their company and assistance in marriage. **(1)**

Bott said that segregated conjugal roles are where husbands and wives have separate social and working lives, and have different responsibilities, and is characterised by a tight-knit network of friends and kin-folk. With joint conjugal roles couples share the domestic work and friends and social life, and they have equal power in the home, this is characterised by loosely-knit networks of kin and friends, where the couple are thrown back onto their own devices. **(2)**

Industrialisation in Great Britain has produced conditions which promote the growth of looser-knit networks, and therefore joint conjugal roles. But communities have also been produced, with 'extreme' industries such as mining, fishing etc. Where, due to lack of education and mobility, close-knit networks of friends and kin develop. Dennis, Henriques and Slaughter in 'Coal Is Our Life', found segregated conjugal roles. The husband's duty was to be the breadwinner, while the wife's life centred around the husband's work. The husband's leisure took place in single-sex peer groups, usually down the pub. Occupation was a major influencing factor on the type of relationship between couples. The existence of segregated conjugal roles was also influenced by the ideology that women are inferior, and not worthy of the same respect as workmates. Tunstall in a similar study entitled 'The Fisherman' found that the exclusively male occupation encouraged segregated roles. While men were at sea, women had sole responsibility in the house, but when the men returned, women had to give up their power and let the man be the 'head of the house'. There was a tightly knit network of friends; men

(1) Wilmott and Young are used to set the answer in a broad historical context. Refer to the changing nature of conjugal roles through this process.

(2) This paragraph clearly defines the key terms in the title.

26

went out with their mates, while women socialised mainly with other women. **(3)**

Joint conjugal relationships are often promoted by the new and expanding towns, where there is a loose network of friends and where people are geographically mobile.

Willmott and Young studied Greenleigh which was a new housing estate in the 1950s. People moved in from the East End of London. Men had to rely on their wives and kids for company and leisure, as they lacked new friends or regular pubs and usually had less money due to having to pay higher rents and rates – this increased home-centredness. Husbands and wives had been cut off from their old close-knit network of friends, and so had to rely on each other for company and assistance. **(4)**

Bott argued that there is a connection between mobility, kin networks and conjugal role relationships. **(5)** Goldthorpe and Lockwood's affluent worker's in their Luton study, found that the workers were geographically mobile and had young families; they were privatised and much leisure-time was spent within the nuclear family.

All the above evidence is a consideration of working class conjugal role relationships. Now, those of the middle class may be examined. **(6)**

Bott argued that because of their greater geographical mobility, middle-class couples are more likely to have joint conjugal role relationships. Willmott and Young argue that joint conjugal roles started in the middle class and are now spreading to the working class.

In the 1960's, Rosser and Harris's study of middle-class couples in Swansea showed that industrialisation has not totally cut the nuclear family off from kin and the extended family. They agree with what Bott said about a connection between conjugal roles and social networks, but say that what happens during married life is more important than the social relationships before it. The degree of domesticity of the wife is a crucial factor in determining what type of relationship is produced.

The process of industrialisation has produced a pattern of increasing looseness of networks and a greater jointness of conjugal role relationships. Criticisms of the above findings are that it all depends on how 'segregated' and 'joint' are defined, as to what results you get. Can jointness be equated with egalitarianism in marriage? **(7)** Gavron in 'The Captive Wife' argued that 62% of working class wives did not know their husbands' income, whereas only one out of the middle-class sample did not know. Therefore, working-class marriages are more likely to be segregated than middle-class ones, but

(3) Good use of two 'classic' studies to highlight segregated conjugal roles in traditional working class occupational communities.

(4) It would have been helpful to use the East London findings for comparison with the Greenleigh sample.

(5) Bott's hypothesis should be more clearly stated here.

(6) A useful link paragraph which clarifies the direction of the argument.

(7) This contrast between 'jointness' and 'egalitarianism' is a crucial issue for consideration in this essay.

Sample Essays

working-class men were more family-minded and home-centred than middle class men.

It is doubtful as to whether there is a link between class and conjugal roles. Willmott and Young studied managing directors and Pahl and Pahl studied directors and found that they spend much more time out of the house, and that their wives had to fit around their husband's work, which produced segregated roles. The relative market power of both partners also determines what type of relationship will develop. **(8)**

Oakley, in 1972, pointed out that while couples may do things jointly, this does not necessarily mean that they do things equally. Little evidence has been found to show an equal division of labour in the home. Willmott and Young found that 21% of men whose wives worked fulltime, 32% of men whose wives worked part-time, and 35% whose wives did not work, gave no help in the home at all. Oakley said that evidence from the 'Symmetrical Family' study does not show equality; she said that 'symmetry remains a myth'. **(9)**

Neither the middle class or working class is characterised by total joint or total segregated marriages, and it is hard to decide which class has the most equal marriage. Willmott and Young's study showed a trend for men to be moving towards home-centredness, but women have been home-centred all along.

Parsons said that in the nuclear family the woman has an expressive role (cleaning, cooking and child-rearing) and the man has an instrumental role – breadwinner, and that this ensures efficient operation of the family. He did not see it as unequal, but as a 'separate but equal' arrangement.

Criticisms of this includes Craddock's study of middle-class couples which showed that women did not specialise in the expressive activity, and that men carried out some instrumental tasks and women did others. Also, Oakley asks in what ways can scrubbing a floor, or cleaning an oven, for example, be seen as an expressive activity. Why is this division of labour necessary and how is it functional? Oakley argues that there is no reason why expressive or instrumental ideas must be done by different people, or why the expressive role has been allocated to the female, and the instrumental role allocated to the male. **(10)**

In conclusion it can be seen that industrialisation did not produce egalitarian relationships in the family. But recent privatisation and women returning to the workplace has changed the nature of conjugal role relationships. But there is no evidence to support the view that marriages are now typically egalitarian or symmetrical. From the above evidence it can also be seen that there is no sharp division

(8) A link could be made to Willmott and Young's stage 4.

(9) Here, effective use of evidence is made to show that the idea of symmetry is really something of a myth.

(10) The functionalist position is criticised well here using Oakley and Craddock.

between the types of role relationships in working-class and middle-class marriages; middle-class marriages are not characterised by joint role relationships, and working-class marriages are not characterised by segregated role relationships, but rather that both classes contain a mixture of both types of relationships. **(11)**

Essay by Julie Adams

(11) The contentiousness of the title is well highlighted.

Structure

The student sets the stage historically referring to Willmott and Young's 4-stage model. Clear definitions of joint and integrated conjugal relations are made early in the essay. Using the 'classic' studies the student highlights the relationship between class and conjugal relations, i.e. working class – segregated, middle class – integrated. The terms integrated and segregated are then brought into contention using Bott and Gavron. More recent studies are then used to point to the changing nature of conjugal roles across classes, thus reinforcing the quotation. An alternative approach might have been to use Willmott and Young's model as the structure around which the above argument could be built.

Overall, a well-structured and very full essay indicating that the student has analysed the question and produced a well-organised response.

Content

The student uses the Greenleigh study but fails to make the most of the comparison with the 'East End'. Bott's hypothesis ought to have been clearly stated in the second paragraph. The student draws upon and uses well, a wide range of important studies to support the argument.

Style

At times a rather staccato approach is adopted. Greater use might have been made of linking paragraphs. However, this is not a major criticism, as generally speaking a 'tight', efficient style is used.

Sample Essays

'In all industrialized countries there is a marked differentiation by gender of most if not all occupations.' (Oakley: *Sex, Gender and Society*) Explain and Discuss.   (AEB June 1983)

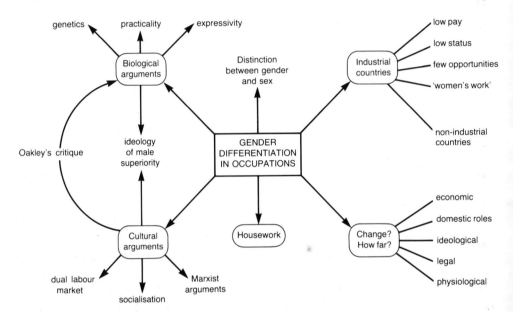

The focus of the answer lies clearly in the gender differentation of occupation in industrialized societies. After making a distinction between gender and sex roles, evidence of gender differences in occupations, both non-manual and manual, could be made. The evidence is drawn mainly from the UK, USA and USSR, although others could be included. Gender differentiation in occupations for women means discrimination *against* women and *for* men, although both are tempered by social class. After pointing out that women are capable of doing 'men's' jobs, using historical examples, the issue of whether or not 'housework' is 'work' can be highlighted. A brief reference to gender roles in non-industrial societies could be used for comparative purposes.

Explanations centre around the biology/culture 'debate'. Exposition of the former could be followed by Oakley's critique. When considering cultural explanations the part played by the agents of socialisation should relate specifically to the creation of gender differentiation in occupations. In particular the generation of the housewife/mother and husband/breadwinner roles should be emphasised. Finally, having established and brought into contention the ideology of male domination, the types, effectiveness of and possibilities for change can be discussed.

'Working-class kids get working-class jobs.' Discuss.

(Cambridge June 1983)

This is an interesting question because it allows, more than most, for the student to draw on a number of sociological areas to compose an answer. It could just be defined as being an 'education' question, but that would be to narrow it down too much. A careful plan will suggest the areas that could be explored.

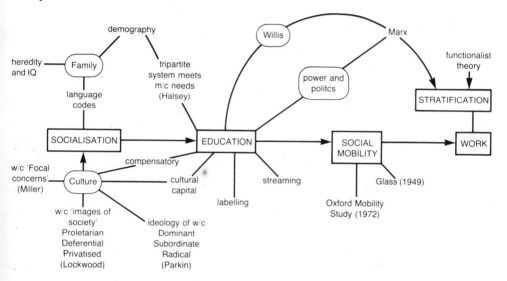

Although education is central to this question, other issues deserve discussion. Social mobility is influenced by demography, and the postwar baby boom meant there were more middle-class children to take advantage of the opportunities of the tripartite system. Are working-class kids socialised differently? Bernstein's work on language codes (and his critics) are relevant, but so are other studies of working-class culture. Miller, Lockwood and Parkin each write about working-class culture, though from rather different perspectives. They could be linked to the 'cultural capital' idea of Bourdieu (criticised by Boudon and his 'positional' theory), and also to the more political dimensions of why the working class accept inequality, and even appear to support it at the polling stations. Willis's imaginative *Learning to Labour* is an important study in this essay, and could be given more prominence than the many other education studies that could be referred to (e.g. Hargreaves, Lacey, Keddie, Young, Ball, Rosenthal and Jacobson, Rist, Rutter, etc). Space should be left to consider the arguments about stratification (functionalist and marxist) and social mobility which relate to the title. A point of feminist sociology could be made at the end: girls are not socialised to get jobs in the same way as boys.

Sample Essays

'The Marxist formulations of the problem of schooling and inequality differ radically from the functionalist theory of educational stratification.' Examine the differences between these two approaches.

(AEB June 1982)

This question requires a contrast between two approaches to education that explain what it does in society, and why, in very different ways. The words 'inequality' and 'stratification' suggest the need to discuss differential educational attatinment and resulting inequalities in stratification and life chances. It is worth noting that education is a 'problem' for marxists in a way that it is not for functionalists.

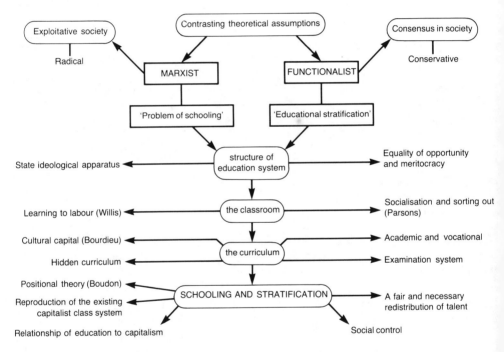

The two approaches could be contrasted step by step all the way through the essay, or through presenting one case being followed by the other. In both perspectives education is seen as having 'functions'. For the functionalist these are things like selection, social control, manpower training and socialisation. For the marxist the function of education is to sustain the current structures of inequality. The mechanisms of this service to the bourgeoisie are largely hidden behind concepts of 'fairness' and 'equality of opportunity', from the marxist point of view.

The marxist approach differs radically because it raises important political questions which are not at all obvious in the functionalist analysis. Both approaches rest on certain theoretical assumptions. The essay should draw on evidence where appropriate. Relevant studies of class differences in attainment (Jackson and Marsden), classroom interaction (Hargreaves, Keddie), labelling (Rist), the relationship of training to jobs (Berg), the operation of the tripartite system (Halsey), could be mentioned briefly.

The recent entrance of the Manpower Services Commission into the field of education, through the Youth Training Scheme (YTS) and Technical and Vocational Education Initiative (TVEI), can be seen as a 'new vocationalism', relating politically to a broadly functionalist view of education.

Sample Essays

'Reporting "news" is inevitably partial, selective and biased.' Discuss with reference to the reporting in the media of areas such as industrial relations, race relations, deviance and political issues.

(AEB June 1982)

The media occupies an interesting and important position in sociological studies, as it is intimately involved in the construction of belief systems, ideology and ways of seeing the world. Only relatively recently has it been seen as 'problematic' in itself, with questions of ownership, control and manipulation being raised. Here 'news' is the central issue, with the idea of impartiality being critically questioned. Two broad viewpoints can be reflected in the answer. One is the liberal perspective which sees the news as factual and neutral. In contrast is the marxist perspective which argues that the news is part of the dominant ideology.

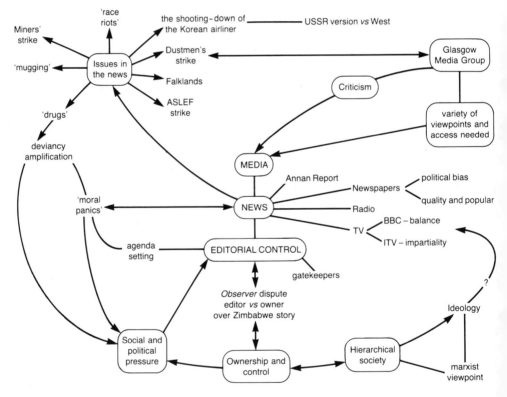

Examples of alleged bias, selectivity and partiality can be given, quoting both actual studies and more up to the moment instances. The editorial control, and entertainment consideration in the 'creation' of the news, means that media are not just neutral mirrors on events. The editor selects news items, the prominence given to them and the way they are presented, acting as a 'gatekeeper', and to an extent as an agenda-setter, for public debate. However, note that the Annan Report suggests that there is 'due impartiality' in this process. While TV and Radio occupy different positions from newspapers, both are subject to pressures. The problem of political pressure and the issue of freedom of information is important. Do such pressures mean that reporting is *inevitably* biased in some way?

Sample Essays

Compare and contrast two major sociological theories of religion and its role in society. (AEB November 1982)

This is a very open question, and could be tackled in a number of different ways. One possibility would be to choose two of the 'founding fathers'. Both Durkheim and Weber gave religion a very prominent place in their theories. Marx had less to say on the subject, but could be used. Alternatively, less universal theories of writers like Wilson (on secularisation), Berger and Luckmann (on religion and the sociology of knowledge) or Bellah (on the individualising of religion) would be appropriate. The question asks the writer to compare and contrast. This does not necessarily mean choosing 'opposite' theories. The answer should be organised around specific concepts: looking at what each theory tries to explain; what are the theory's assumptions about society; what types of explanation are offered (with what evidence); where do the theories differ, and so on. The role of religion in society, as seen by the different theories again can be compared and contrasted. In the discussion a distinction might be drawn between religion as a practice and system of beliefs, and religion as an organisation (i.e. churches, denominations, sects). In the 'map' that follows the theories of Weber and Durkheim are used.

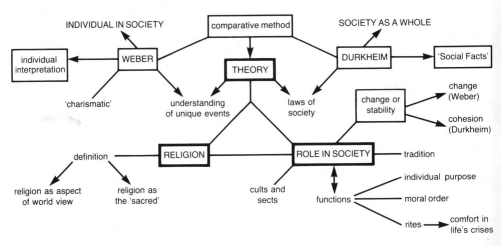

Contrasting Weber and Durkheim provides much material for discussion. The different view about the individual, society, and the nature of sociological knowledge could be contrasted, and illustrated with their ideas on religion. The marxist perspective, with the relationship of religion to ideology, and conflict in and through religion, would also deserve brief attention, possibly in a conclusion.

Does the increasing popularity of fringe religious groups indicate that secularisation is a myth?   (Oxford May 1983)

'Fringe religions' refers to sects and cults that have increasingly come into prominence, some like the Moonies, obtaining considerable wealth and political power, others, like the People's Temple, acquiring extraordinary influence over their members. The discussion will need to clarify the various definitions of secularisation, and outline the different levels of organisation of religious activity. A distinction should be drawn between religion as church activity and religion as individual experience. The issue is fundamentally one of how the concept of 'secularisation' is to be operationalised.

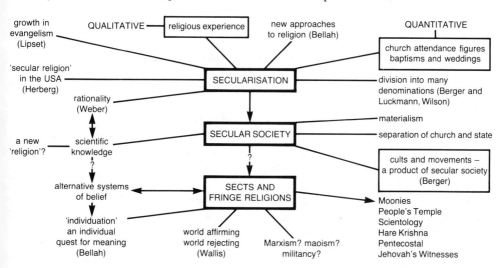

If secularisation is defined in terms of a decline in church power and attendance, and a fragmentation of religious institutions, then secularisation is occurring in Europe. If the outlook and ideals of secular life are invading church organisation, then secularisation is occurring in the USA even with its high church membership. Should religion just be defined in terms of church membership or attendance? A broader definition that takes account of strength of belief, or claims to individual experience will open up the debate. The role of fringe religious groups in this broader definition of religion should be explored. Various categorisations of cults and sects have been suggested (Wilson; Wallis). The contention that they are 'increasingly popular' should be assessed. One or two could be looked at in some detail. In a secular society are the passionate beliefs of some in certain political ideologies also a symptom of secularism, or part of a search for religion?

Sample Essays

'The links between social class and voting behaviour were never straightforward but in recent years the traditional patterns have increasingly broken down'. Discuss.

(AEB November 1983)

Traditionally, people voted according to their class (the middle class – m/c – vote Tory, and the working class – w/c – vote Labour). Voters are seen to be rational in liberal democratic theory. Voting according to class is seen to be the 'normal' vote, but a large proportion of 'deviant' voters (those who do not vote according to class) exists; for example, one-third of the w/c vote Tory, and one-fifth of the m/c vote Labour. **(1)**

(1) The opening paragraph is of immediate relevance to the question. The lack of fit between class and voting, traditionally, is clearly highlighted here.

The relationship between subjective class (what people define themselves as, i.e. w/c or m/c) and voting behaviour, is even stronger than that between objective class (e.g. as defined by the Registrar General, m/c are nonmanual workers, w/c are manual workers). Butler and Stokes said that between 1952 and 1962 the objective w/c vote for Labour never rose above 58%. Weber suggests, therefore, that we need to ask why someone's subjective class differs from what might be objectively expected. **(2)**

(2) Class is defined and the important distinction between objective and subjective class and voting behaviour is evidenced using Butler and Stokes.

One explanation, is that the dominant institutions of a society embody conservative and m/c values and therefore, all classes become socialised into these values. Parkin states that he finds it surprising that in a generally conservative society two-thirds of the w/c do still vote Labour. He sees these two-thirds of the w/c as the 'deviants', as they do not conform to society's dominant norms. W/c subcultures provide protective barriers, where different norms and values from the dominant ones can be fostered (e.g. socialist ones). These form a 'cultural buffer'. **(3)**

(3) A succinct summary of Parkin.

Goldthorpe and Lockwood in analysing w/c voting patterns, divide the w/c into two main groups: traditionalists and instrumental collectivists. The latter vote Labour and support the trade unions, but not out of loyalty or solidarity, but for what they can get out of them. Their vote is instrumentally motivated, and will be changed if it is in their best interest to do so. Traditionalists can be subdivided into: proletarian traditionalists (who are the most radical and class-conscious), and deferential traditionalists (defined later on).

McKenzie and Silver also divide the w/c into two groups: deference voters (Goldthorpe and Lockwoods' traditionalists), who prefer 'socially superior' leaders and so therefore vote Tory; and secular voters who are young and well-paid and whose vote is instrumentally motivated, and so may vote Tory.

But Goldthorpe and Lockwood refute the embourgeoisement thesis by saying that these instrumental voters are not becoming m/c. Butler and Rose said that after the 1959 election (when Labour lost its third election in a row), that affluent workers were identifying with m/c values, voting Tory, and therefore becoming m/c. This view was strongly criticised by Nordlinger who said that the w/c Tories were more satisfied with their levels of pay and that satisfaction leads to a desire to maintain the status quo. As the Tory Party has a traditional image, these people vote for them. **(4)** But there may be some truth in the emborgeoisement thesis, as in 1979, and again in 1983, there was a strong swing of affluent worker voters from Labour to Tory. Goldthorpe and Lockwood, and McKenzie and Silver, argue that the instrumental voter is likely to switch his vote if it is in his best interest to do so. **(5)**

The number of m/c deviant voters is not so great – only one-fifth. Raynor divides these into two groups. Firstly, the 'intellectual left'. This group has a wide education and knowledge. It has been argued that their wide education enables them to see beyond their own needs, and to sympathize with the disadvantaged. Secondly, 'those with low status within the m/c'. These people rank higher in education and qualifications then they do in status. He says that the resulting resentment is shown in the affiliation to a radical political party. They vote Labour out of pique and insecurity. Parkin strongly criticises Raynor, by saying that low status jobs are the result of radical political ideas and not vice-versa.

A third group can be identified: the 'sons of the affluent workers', as Goldthorpe calls them. The have continued to support Labour even after their socio-economic rise in status. This partly reflects loyalty to their roots, but it may also be that Labour now presented policies that potentially widen its basis of support. **(6)**

In recent years, the traditional vote according to a person's class has eroded, and the study of the 1983 election by Crewe illustrated this fact. The Labour Party still has the support of the traditional w/c (those in traditional jobs such as the mining industry) – communities which are in fast decline, but this is a declining group. Labour has lost the 'new w/c', the affluent w/c voter. Amongst trade unionists, Labour was only 7% ahead of the Tories. Affluent workers who own their own house, or who live in the south-east, put Labour third, behind the Alliance. The Alliance (Liberal/SDP) emerged a few years earlier and was predominant in this election. It's vote was spread evenly across the classes. It was the m/c who showed strong class consciousness and solidarity by voting Tory. The decline of the w/c vote for Labour makes its claim to be the party of the w/c increasingly threadbare. 'The transformation of w/c partisanship over the

(4) A competent and comprehensive run through the 1950s and 1960s material mentioning the different types of deviant voters.

(5) A crucial link to the question here. The student brings the answer into the '70s and '80s with reference to the last two elections, emphasising the applicability of the concept of 'instrumentalism' to this period.

(6) Comprehensive coverage of the middle-class 'deviant' voter.

Sample Essays

last 25 years, must rank as the most significant change, in the post-war period, of the social basis in British politics' as said by Crewe. In summary, the 1983 election showed the tremendous volatility of the electorate, and that there is an erosion of traditional social class support for the major parties. **(7)**

The above evidence shows that class isn't the only influencing factor: age, region, gender, religion and race also play an important part. **(8)**

Goldthorpe and Lockwood, Butler, and Stokes strongly reject the view that the old are 'naturally' more conservative, and that the young are 'naturally more radical'. King explains it in terms of 'political generations'. This concept has been updated by Crewe, who said that in the 1983 election the 65+ age group were markedly less conservative, as they first voted in 1945 when there was a landslide victory for Labour, and so that is where their loyalties have remained. Also, Crewe showed that youth were not necessarily radical in 1983; most young people did not vote Labour. Youth is particularly equated with apathy in 1983, as 32% of new voters did not bother to vote.

Gender also plays an important part in voting behaviour. Generally women tend to be more conservative than men, usually because they do not experience the radicalising effect of industrial conflict and the associated affiliation to the Labour Party. But in 1979, an equal number of men and women voted Tory, and Crewe's study showed that in 1983 less women than men voted Tory.

Race is becoming increasingly important in voting in the U.S. and U.K. Usually ethnic minorities vote left of centre. In 1983, many did not bother to vote at all, and Labour was hit by this.

Religion is another important factor when considering patterns of voting behaviour. King stated that 'the C of E is still, to a most remarkable degree, the Tory party at prayer'.

Butler and Stokes (1963) showed that out of church-attending Anglicans, 72% were Tories. Church-going is associated with conservatism. Catholics are an exception to this rule, as they have historically favoured the more left wing parties. **(9)**

All of these factors are related to class, and some can be linked together. **(10)**

In conclusion it can be said that there is an element of individual choice in voting. This is particularly clear in the case of floating voters (who are the least educated and worst informed part of the electorate). They almost appear to vote at random. Heading says that recently there has been an erosion of traditional party – class allegiances, and that people are tending to vote more instrumentally; they will vote for the party that offers them the most at a given time.

(7) This paragraph captures (a) the decline in traditional Labour support; (b) the emergence and impact of the 'Alliance'; and (c) the volatility of the electorate. It directly answers the question, demonstrating the recent changes in traditional voting patterns.

(8) A useful linking p:ragraph that prevents the reader getting lost in the detail of the essay.

(9) In this latter part of the essay traditional material on 'other factors' is presented and updated by quoting Crewe's analysis.

(10) This sentence suggests the complex nature of the relationship between these 'other factors' and social class.

The 1983 election clearly illustrated that people are no longer voting according to class as strongly as in the past, but that they are voting instrumentally. **(11)**

(11) The conclusion raises the idea of individual choice, relating it to the 'floating voter' and 'instrumentalism' and at the same time pointing to the weakening of traditional class–party allegiance.

Essay by Julie Adams

Structure

This is a well-structured essay. The student clearly states the traditional pattern of class and voting behaviour, defining the key concepts on the way. Traditional material is dealt with first, highlighting the lack of a straightforward fit between class and voting behaviour, using the 'working-class Tory' voter and middle-class Labour voter as examples. In the latter part of the essay recent changes are contrasted with the past, and the changing influence of factors other than class are developed. The student summarises well, drawing on the preceding discussion, introducing the ideas of individual choice and 'instrumentalism' and noting a weakening of the class – party link.

Content

The student makes very good use of the selected material. Greater emphasis might have been placed on the changing class structure and class imagery (Roberts). Here, the link between one's place and view of work and voting behaviour could be developed. The ideas of 'retrospective' and 'issue' voting are also important to this essay. Brief mention could be made of the marxist perspective which suggests the futility of parliamentary democracy in a capitalist society. On the whole, a wide range of research is clearly and succinctly presented in the 45 minute time-limit.

Style

Stylistically, the essay is clear and concise. The argument progresses logically, with adequate links between points and no sudden 'jumps'.

Sample Essays

Is the concept of a 'power elite' relevant to understanding contemporary British politics?   (Oxford May 1982)

This question raises the issue of how power is exercised, who by and in whose interest in British society. Furthermore, issues of theory and method emerge, as different theoretical positions using different methods of research draw different conclusions.

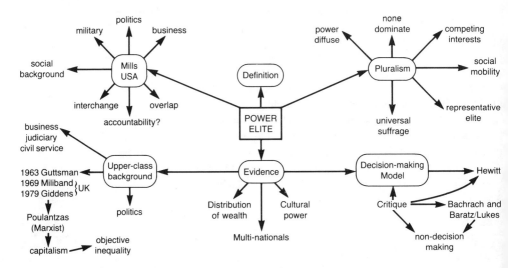

After a tentative definition (Meisel), a consideration of the theoretical and methodological background to the 'power elite' question can be made. Empirical evidence is clearly linked to the theoretical positions. Hewitt uses Dahl's 'Decision-Making Model' and concludes that power is diffuse. Guttsman, Miliband and Giddens look at the social class background of the 'power elite' and find them largely drawn from upper-class backgrounds. This, they argue, is evidence of a ruling class, indeed a 'power elite'. The decision-making approach is weakened by Bachrach and Baratz whilst Poulantzas undermines the social background model. Other evidence can be drawn upon to criticise the pluralists, e.g. the limited redistribution of wealth, the emergence and concentration of multi-national corporations, and the influence of cultural power, e.g. education and the mass media. The concept of a 'power elite' is relevant to understanding contemporary British politics but methodological limitations limit its use. It is as difficult for the marxists as it is for the power elite theorists to establish, empirically, that they rule in their interests. Despite such limitations, the past century has seen an increasing concentration of power in the British political economy. Whether this is seen in conspiratorial terms or in terms of system constraints will depend upon the theoretical and methodological position taken.

The paradox of the sociology of the community is the existence of a body of theory which constantly predicts the collapse of community, and a body of empirical studies which finds community alive and well.' (Abrams: *Work, Urbanism and Inequality*). Explain and discuss.

(AEB June 1983)

After explaining the concept of community, the meaning of the 'collapse of community' and the rural–urban debate, the problem is one of being spoiled for choice. There are so many theorists that could be mentioned on one side (Durkheim, Tönnies, Simmel, Wirth, Parsons) with empirical studies to back them up (Burgess, Redfield, Whyte, Willmott and Young). There is also a wealth of research to support the claim that communities are not collapsing in industrial cities (e.g. Gans, Willmott and Young, Colin Bell) or that the idea of a rural – urban continuum is of doubtful use (Lewis, Newby, Pahl). The answer could explore the way in which empirical research has been influenced by the values of the researchers and how theory has had to be modified to cope with actual findings.

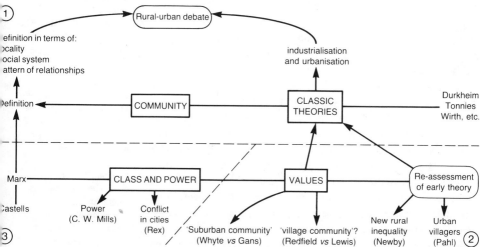

A list of names and brief mention of lots of studies, in no particular order, will not get great credit. By using the clue of the gap between theory and research, and the question of the values of the sociologists that can give rise to this contradication, the debate can be made quite broad. The centre-piece would be on the contradictory findings (e.g. Redfield *vs* Lewis) and the re-assessment of earlier community theory. The third area, relating to Marx, would be referred to at the end, as he argued that community could only exist within classes (Castells) This allows discussion of the more conflict-based ideas of Rex and Moore, and also C. W. Mills (see Lee and Newby *The Problem of Sociology*, 1983, for a summary of many community studies).

Sample Essays

What have been the main consequences of colonialism for the industrialised and underdeveloped worlds? (Cambridge June 1982)

The legacy of colonialism has had a major impact on the industrialised nations of the North as well as the under-developed worlds in the South. The British, French and Dutch colonised lands in Africa, Asia and Latin America. The effect of the spread of capitalism has had, from one point of view, disastrous consequences for the under-developed nations. A major feature of colonialism has been its distorting effect on the economies and political structures of the South.

Colonialism exploited human labour reserves in the under-developed worlds and particularly in Africa. (Williams (1972), Dumont (1966) and Rodney (1972) examined the slave trade in Africa, and concluded that colonialism drained Africa of much of its skilled labour power. There are further examples of how colonialism had major consequences – for example, the British, French and Dutch mining in South Africa. After all, many underdeveloped nations are rich in minerals which the indigenous population cannot extract. Colonialism changed this relationship, and the reserves of the South came 'to benefit trade in the North'. **(1)**

The theory that surrounds this explanation of development is exploitation or dependency theory, and it examines the way in which the North/South relationship operates as a result of colonialism. Marxists and neo-Marxists view the relationship in terms of conflict and set it in a context of the nature of capitalism. **(2)** Colonialism revolves around a relationship of power which establishes a dependency of the under-developed world on the industrialised North. This concept of core – periphery or metropolis – satellite, put forward by Seidman and Friedmann examines the nature of trade. Trading links were established, as a result of colonialism, which precipitated economic dependency of the South on the North. The South exports low-cost raw materials whereas the North exports high-cost manufactured goods. In this way a relationship of economic dependency develops at the expense of the South. **(3)**

Neo-colonialism, then, has built upon this economic dependency initiated in part by colonial powers. Sociologists such as Frank have commentated on this relationship of power and exploitation. Indeed, the South has found that it is affected by the North not only economically but politically as well. **(4)**

H. Ushewokunze in 'Zimbabwe: Problems and Prospects of Socialist Development' (1982) argued that the link with capitalism

(1) Colonialism is dealt with in these opening paragraphs in terms of 'the spread of capitalism', the 'slave trade in Africa' and the wish 'to benefit trade in the North'. A few more historical points would help, for instance mentioning how contact with Europeans often undermined aspects of the colonies' culture, e.g. the colonisation of India and the destruction of its textile industry. Colonialism often involved stereotyping of the colonised as 'savage', 'unintelligent', 'pagan'; the racialist overtones of these descriptions still persist today.

(2) This is a useful point. The marxist analysis that can be applied within countries is here being applied to international relations. It is helpful to note that the same arguments that supported nineteenth-century capitalism were used, and one still partly used, to support colonisation.

(3) Brief, but adequate, summary of a particular theory about the relationship of 'North' to 'South'. The point could be made that the cause of this economic dependency of the South is normally seen as self-caused, rather than a product of the relationship with the North.

impeded true socialist development. Further, foreign investments were inherent in the Zimbabwean economy (for example, Hippo Valley for sugar). Therefore, the subtle link with the North extends far beyond the influence of colonialism and H. Ushewokunze would argue that there is still a relationship between Zimbabwe and Britain (for example, **(5)** agreements were made during the Lancaster House conferences that effectively gave Britain some degree of control over land use).

This argument contrasts with the functionalist inspired modernisation theory put forward by Talcott Parsons and Walt Rostow. Rostow's analysis of the 'drive to maturity' cannot be achieved with external influence which is part of the legacy of colonialism. **(6)** Economies in the Third World have been distorted and shaped by the demands of capitalism – for example, Cuba produces sugar, sisal is produced in Tanzania and copper in Zambia. In this way there can be no 'development' independent of external factors, which tends to be ignored when considering the solutions to the problems of the Third World.

T. Hayter in 'The Creation of World Poverty: An Alternative View to the Brandt Report', argues that European expansionism had a devastating effect for the Third World. Further, colonialism benefited only the West and had a destructive impact on the South. Hayter, like Frank, sets her arguments against the backcloth of capitalism **(7)** and claims that only socialism can remedy the damage done by imperialism.

Brandt also examined the nature of the North/South relationship and he argued that by stimulating growth in the Third World markets would be created in the North. Brandt aimed to achieve a symbiotic relationship which was based on both moral and economic grounds. It could be seen that colonialism had distorted this relationship by establishing an unequal balance of power. After all, coercion is still used as a method by colonial powers, and also through superpower involvement – for example, the American invasion of Grenada, and the British defence of the Falklands. **(8)**

However, the superpowers are keen to distance themselves from accusations of colonialism (especially in the Third World), precisely because of the damaging effect it has had on the North/South relationship. Independence, for many under-developed states, has been coupled with an inbred reluctance to trust the motives of the industrialised West. In this way colonialism may have benefited the North economically but politically it was damaging.

Therefore, colonialism and the development of neo-colonialism has had a major impact on the industrialised west and the under-

(4) This sentence makes a link between the economic analysis just dealt with, and political points about to be considered.

(5) Ushewokunze (quoted in O'Donnell, 1983) is a Zimbabwean socialist, in their government, and so provides a Third World viewpoint. There is not room for much detail, but it is valuable to slip in an example or two, as this paragraph does.

(6) Here the description is too brief. A few sentences more on the assumptions of modernisation theory, and the expectation that the Third World should follow the pattern of economic development of the west, would be helpful.

(7) The essay maintains its link to this key concept of capitalism and its effects, while managing to mention the important Brandt Report, and its critic, T. Hayter.

(8) It is always beneficial to give brief, up-to-date examples of points being made.

developed nations. Further, it has influenced the nature of the North/South relationship which cannot be repaired with diplomacy alone.

Essay by Fran Lemon

Structure

The essay is built around an analysis of the spread of capitalism, mentioned in the opening paragraphs. The different arguments are well linked, and the contrast between modernisation theories and exploitation theories is made clear. Whether this is the best way of organising this essay is open to debate, because while relevant it is not specifically answering the question set.

Content

More space should be given to looking at the consequences of colonialism, both for developed and less developed countries. Aspects that might be mentioned: the pattern of trade links and economic structures (the idea that western economic institutions and analysis are inappropriate, as argued by Polly Humphries, is important), multi-nationals, poverty and malnutrition, rapid urbanisation, health and disease, and even the so-called population explosion (which Susan George argues is caused in no small way by inequalities of wealth and life chances). The attitudes and racialism of the North are also a product of colonialism.

Style

This is good. It is clear, with points well divided into linked paragraphs, making good use of brief examples.

Distinguish between crime and deviance. Why are some deviant acts classified as criminal and others not? (Oxford May 1982)

There would appear to be two parts to this question. The first consisting of a definition of crime in relation to deviance, and the second analysing the criminality or otherwise of different types of deviance. Yet important sociological points are raised even in the apparently straightforward first part. The definition of crime does not present much of a problem to sociologists. One possibility is: 'An intended activity defined as harmful to the public welfare; banned by a specifically criminal law and open to prosecution'.

However the definition of deviance is far from straightforward, and many contradictory concepts abound, e.g. 'statistically uncommon behaviour' (Wilkins); 'a quality of the socially unsuccessful' (Douglas); 'creative innovation which is as yet unestablished' (Parsons); 'that which Everyman identifies as deviant'(Berger). (See M. Mann, *The Macmillan Student Encyclopedia of Sociology*, 1983, for more detail.) The simple Becker typology might be a useful guide to defining deviance.

The second part of the essay raises the question of who sets the laws, and who has the power to classify acts as deviant or not.

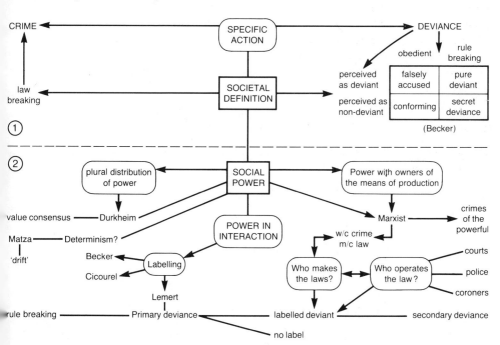

Labelling theory could be critically reviewed, as an approach to the way in which power operates. Alternative viewpoints on the power dimension could

Sample Essays

be illustrated by contrasting the more functionalist analysis with marxist/conflict positions. The role of the police and the courts in defining crime could be discussed (using J. Young, S. Cohen, A. Cicourel, P. Rock, S. Hall, etc.).

Durkheim attempted to show that sociology could contribute to the understanding of suicide. How far was he successful?

(AEB June 1982)

This question requires more than just an essay on Durkheim's approach to suicide; it asks for a critical account of how far sociology, as Durkheim conceived of it, could explain suicide. Therefore, the approach Durkheim took to sociology, as well as alternative approaches, needs to be assessed, along with their appropriateness for explaining the highly individual act of suicide.

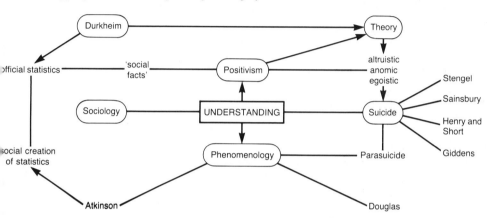

Some discussion of the statistical material used by Durkheim, showing the stability of suicide rates in overseas countries, and amongst certain social groups (even up to the present day) could be stated. It was on this regularity and pattern of social acts that Durkheim based his argument for social facts: 'ways of acting, thinking and feeling that exist outside the individual consciousness'. This positivistic type of explanation he elaborated with his discussions of suicide as related to the degree of integration of the individual into society (altruistic, egoistic, anomic).

Another theory which shows features of Durkheim's approach is Sainsbury's ecological study of suicide in London. Henry and Short (quoted in Cotgrove) argue that suicide is a response to frustration. Giddens states that there is a need for the 'ego ideal' to be taken into account. In other words some psychological factors have to be recognised.

The statistical basis of Durkheim's argument has been criticised, and these criticisms could form the conclusions of the essay. Stengel demonstrates the need to look at why methods of suicide have changed (e.g. the introduction of non-poisonous natural gas). Douglas and Atkinson separately show that suicide statistics are themselves socially created and far from 'social facts'. The stress the need for a more phenomenological approach to sociology. Parasuicide could also be discussed.

Sample Essays

'The establishment of the Welfare State represents the single most important attempt to change the social structure of British society this century.' Explain and discuss.   (AEB June 1984)

The first consideration of this essay is to define what is meant by the Welfare State (see M. Mann, *The Macmillan Student Encyclopedia of Sociology*, 1983). The Welfare State is composed of five main parts: Education, Health, Housing, Social Security and Community Care Services. Any definition should raise the issue of state intervention in the life of the individual, bringing into contention the principles of 'freedom' and 'equality'. The Fabian 'gradualist approach' to social change adopted by the Labour Party should be mentioned. The answer should be structured around a clear historical perspective. Also, what is meant by change in social structure should be outlined, e.g. social mobility, class formation, life chances, etc.

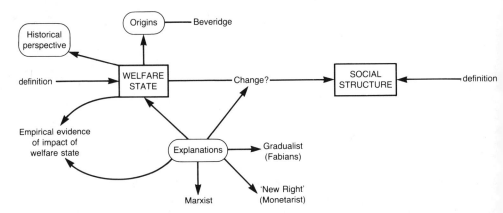

Has the Welfare State changed the social structure of British society? A growing body of evidence suggests otherwise: poverty (Townsend); distribution of income and wealth (Diamond; Westergaard and Resler); access to medical care, education and housing subsidies (Le Grande). It has been suggested that even redistribution of wealth through social security payments is tempered by high unemployment (Stephenson).

Marxists criticise the gradualists and argue that the Wefare State is (a) a remedy for the worst depredations of capitalism, (b) an agency of repression, and (c) a source of jobs for the middle classes. The inequitable capitalist system remains intact despite this tampering (Gough).

Other criticisms of the Welfare State which could be mentioned come from the 'New Right' movement in the Conservative Party of the late 1970s and 1980s. They argue that the public sector 'lives off' the private sector, which is the real wealth-creator. To balance the books cuts have to be made in services. The family is seen as the alternative to the expensive and inef-

ficient Welfare State. It could be noted that whereas in the Beveridge pro-
posals the economy is seen as the servant of the political system, with this
'monetarist' approach, the state, in part, becomes the servant of the free-
market capitalist economy. Pressure is exerted to privatise in health and education, and women are portrayed as wives and mothers in a traditional
(repressive?) sense (Fitzgerald).

The evidence seems to suggest that the Welfare State has had a limited
role in changing British social structure. It is suggested that other factors
in the capitalist industrial structure have played a greater part (Giddens;
Dahrendorf; Goldthorpe and Llewellyn).

Sample Essays

'Choice of method in sociological research reflects among other things, theoretical assumptions and practical restraints.' In the light of this statement, compare postal questionaires and face-to-face interviews as methods of social research. (AEB June 1982)

The quotation highlights the fact that both theory and practical problems influence the choice of a particular method of research. Both these aspects will need to be investigated and illustrated when comparing postal questionnaires and face-to-face interviews. The findings of the research and the data generated will vary considerably depending on the method that is chosen. Theoretical assumptions can refer to more than just specific theories about given topics, as they can apply to assumptions about the nature of sociological research itself.

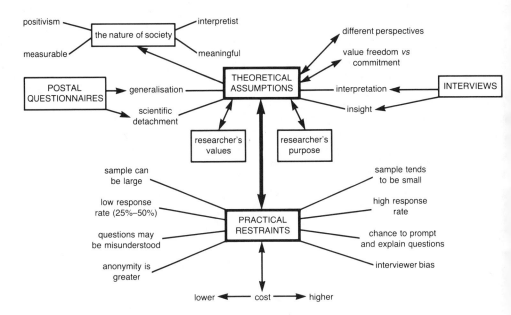

An answer should emphasise that the purpose of research is influenced by, and in turn may influence, theoretical assumptions. Market-research may rest on different assumptions to research into unemploymert. In particular, the view that the social world is measurable and quantifiable should be contrasted with the view that the interpretations of participants in social action need to be considered. The problem of the researcher influencing his/her research (Heisenberg's uncertainty principle) needs discussion.

A central point raised by this question is that of the reliability and validity of methods chosen, and how even these concepts take on a different complexion depending on the theoretical starting-point. The large sample in the postal questionnaire has to be balanced against the possibility of considerable bias in those who actually respond. The opportunity of greater depth in interviews must be assessed against the probability mentioned should be outlined and contrasted in terms of their advantages and practical limitations. Some features will be similar in parts (e.g., design of the questionnaire or question schedule), and differ in other parts (e.g. complexity, open or closed questions).

Illustration of the points made from appropriate studies is desirable (e.g. the census, *Which?* questionnaires to members, Blauner's questionnaire on alienation; Goldthorpe and Lockwood's *Affluent Worker* study, Becker's interviews with teachers, Oakley's various studies of women, etc.)

Sample Essays

synopsis

'The sociologist's perspective of the social system has been developed to a large extent by borrowing from the perspectives of the natural sciences, originally from biology and mechanics'. What are the advantages and disadvantages of borrowing from these perspectives?
(AEB June 1980)

Sociologists have drawn on the perspectives of the natural sciences in order to develop the biological and mechanical analogies **(1)**. An analogy is a model used to conceptualise social reality, and so the advantage of developing these analogies is that they help to describe and explain the complexity of the social system. **(2)**

Firstly, the biological analogy views society as a living organism and was developed by Herbert Spencer. **(3)** Spencer built on Comte's positivistic and holistic view of society in terms of growth, structure, the mutual dependence of the parts and the life of a society being more prolonged than that of its component parts. In this way the complexity of the social system can be understood in terms of three functions – regulation, distribution and sustenance. **(4)**

So the biological analogy compares society to that of a living organism and therefore links the natural sciences to that of social science. In terms of growth, for example, Spencer drew on Darwin's ideas of a human life-cycle since societies are also part of a cycle of evolution, maturity and possibly collapse (such as the Roman Empire). Animals, too, evolve and become more specialised and complex. In this way, the growth and development in nature can be compared to the growth and evolution of societies. **(5)**

The biological analogy also helps the social scientist to understand the structure of societies, and the British anthropologist, Radcliffe-Brown, developed the functionalist concept, by studying small societies in terms of functions. He concluded that the functional nature of social activity is analogous to that of living organisms. Further, he emphasised the continuity of the social structure despite the death of particular individuals. The advantages of the biological analogy can be seen in terms of growth and structure when attempting to explain and understand the social system. **(6)**

Another aspect of the biological analogy is that of equilibrium. In the natural science of biology, homeostasis occurs, and Walter Cannon developed the idea of regulation maintaining a steady state in his book 'The Wisdom of the Body' (1963). This biological concept of homeostasis then was developed as part of the social sciences by Talcott Parsons who argued that homeostatic mechanisms maintained the norms of society – for example, 'dysfunctions' in society were regulated by homeostatic mechanisms, such as more police

'(1) The opening sentence usefully states what the question is essentially about.

(2) An analogy is a 'model', as suggested here; a fuller definition would emphasise that it draws on something familiar (e.g. a living organism) that shows features with something less familiar or obvious (e.g. society).

(3) It could be mentioned in passing that he wrote in the 19th century.

(4) This paragraph mentions a number of relevant ideas in a clear and concise way.

(5) Instead of going into detail on each aspect of the analogy, one is taken as an illustration. It would not be advisable to put equal detail on all the features of this analogy, for there would not be time to do justice to other parts of the question.

(6) It could be more clearly stated that Radcliffe-Brown used the idea of 'structure' to analyse simple societies. His inductive anthropological techniques are called 'structural-functionalism'.

in troubled areas. **(7)** The advantage of this approach is that it helps understand the nature of the social system and its maintenance.

However, there are disadvantages when considering the biological analogy. Firstly, it rests on the assumption that the growth of society is both inevitable and irresistible. It also assumes that existing society is in the stage of inevitable development. Further, it assumes that society is held together by a 'skin' of moral values and codes – a concept which Durkheim called consensus or the 'collective conscience'.

Spencer also points out disadvantages of borrowing from the perspectives of the natural sciences, especially that of biology. He argues there are significant differences between the nature of society and a living organism. Firstly, society is not a continuous mass and members of society have mobility – indeed, all parts of society have mobility. Also, all members of society have feeling which is not true of living organisms.

Further criticisms of the biological analogy include the claim that it is a tautological argument. **(8)** Marxists also argue that the analogy underplays conflict and there is no explanation of change.

The quote refers to borrowing from the perspective of mechanics. The mechanical analogy includes the view of society as a team. However, the disadvantage of this is that it assumes there is a goal to be achieved and that the members of society are united in achieving that goal.

The mechanical analogy also includes the cybernetic model which views society as a self-regulating machine – for example regulating mechanisms would include the police, army and political system. An example of the mechanistic approach **(9)** is the model provided by Talcott Parsons of adaptation, goal attainment, integration and latency.

The marxist perspective particularly criticises this functionalist approach of seeing society as a machine – for example, Dennis Wrong argues such an approach leads to an 'oversocialised view of man'. **(10)**

The main advantage of borrowing from the natural sciences for Comte was the fact that it helped moves to establish sociology as a positivistic and recognised 'science'. However, critics argue that such biological and mechanical analogies present a simplistic view of the social system since there are differences between society and the nature of the natural sciences. The biological and mechanical analogies should therefore be seen as providing insight but not being a total explanation of the nature of the social system. **(11)**

Essay by Fran Lemon

(7) So far each paragraph effectively builds on the one preceeding it. The point made about the use of police in troubled areas does illustrate the idea of a homeostatic mechanism. Where possible it is a good technique to use examples to back up arguments. Other specific examples could be used here.

(8) Clarification of this key criticism is necessary.

(9) The mechanical analogy could have been introduced earlier in the essay. Now there is not much time to develop it, and really consider the question.

(10) This does establish one disadvantage of using these analogies, which could be dealt with in greater detail. It should be noted however, that Dennis Wrong is not a marxist.

(11) In the final paragraph the central point of the question is taken up: 'What are the advantages and disadvantages . . .?' This should have come rather earlier in the essay.

Sample Essays

Structure

Overall this essay is quite well constructed. The introduction is clear and appropriate. The two analogies are developed in a logical way, before the concluding section which considers specific disadvantages. The weakness is the amount of space devoted to the biological analogy at the expense of other parts of the questions.

Content

Not enough is said about the mechanical analogy. The idea of 'teams' and 'self-regulating machines' should be explored. More needs to be presented in general about borrowing from the 'perspectives of the natural sciences'. The positivistic scientific method may not be appropriate for studying people who have self-consciousness, and endeavour to interpret their situation. This approach has tended also to emphasise consensus in society and the validity of the 'status quo'. The 'reification' of society through this model should be critically assessed.

Specific examples could be taken to illustrate the application of these analogies, e.g. Davis and Moore on stratification or Parsons on education.

Style

The style is a strong point of this essay because most paragraphs manage to deal with quite a lot of material, but in a succinct way. The parts of the essay are well linked together, and the answer is coherent.

Many arguments about the non-scientific character of sociology are based upon a mistaken view of the logic, the methods and the procedures of natural scientists'. Explain and discuss.

(AEB June 1984)

This question may be misinterpreted to be an 'Is sociology a science'? Question. This is clearly not the case. The question requires a consideration of the range of views about the natural sciences which brings into contention their logic, methods and procedures.

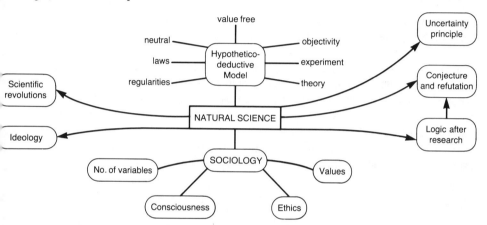

After a brief description of the hypothetico-deductive method, a number of variations and criticisms can be considered. For Popper, scientific method progresses through conjecture and refutation, consequently all knowledge provisional. However, it has been argued that the logic of science only emerges after research is completed (Kaplan, Watson). For Kuhn, scientists (like sociologists) operate through sets of assumptions (paradigms) about what the natural world is like, which may dominate, their research, irrespective of contradictory evidence. When this evidence becomes too great to ignore 'scientific revolution' ensues (e.g. Copernicus).

Ideology can be seen to intrude in what the scientist researches and how is used. (Rose and Rose, Gomm.). Heisenberg's 'uncertainty principle' highlights how the scientist can influence the behaviour observed. The stereotypical view of natural science method has now been brought into contention. Accusations of the nonscientific character of sociology revolve around the 'uncontrollable' number of variables; the 'consciousness' of the subject matter; ethical problems; and the intrusion of values. Positivist and interpretavist methodologies can be highlighted around these points. Many of the criticisms of sociology as non-scientific are based on a particular view of science. However, this view of science has been shown to be highly contentious, thus reducing the impact of those criticisms against sociology.

The examination

At the end of your course, you will want to get the best result you can. Techniques of successful preparation for the examination can go a long way to improving grades, and some simple principles can be applied with success. We will look at revision, surviving 'exam nerves' and making the best use of your time in the examination room.

Revision

Good notes
Your revision will be aided by having made good notes throughout your course. These should not be too detailed, but must be accurate. If set out neatly with intelligent use of colour for underlining and 'highlight' pens for important parts, they will be easier to learn from and recall. It is never too early to start making extra notes around a topic, to back up class work. The more familiar you are with the material the easier it will be to learn.

Card system
Many of our students have found that keeping a card system, on which brief summaries of specific studies are recorded, is very valuable. Small file cards are ideal. They can be used to revise from, and can ensure that you actually remember key studies in the exam rather than having them on the 'tip of your tongue'.

Plan for revision
The revision period should start several months prior to the exam. You should plan what you are going to revise, and when, and draw up a schedule. Try to go over everything at least three times. The first time is to ensure that you notes are complete, and that you understand the ideas and arguments. The second time you should put maximum effort into learning the material. The third time is to check what you know, and to relearn what has not yet been memorised.

For the final month or two make a detailed day-by-day plan of the topics you are going to revise. In this way you will know what you have to revise on any particular day, and you will know that you have time to complete all your revision. Remember to schedule in some blank days or times, to catch up, if you get behind.

Be active
You will remember best what has actively gone through your mind. Don't just read through your notes. Close your file and verbally summarise the key ideas, or write them out. Make summaries of all the key points on a particular area, using colour, boxes, underlining, and anything else that will help make

them visually distinctive and memorable. Mind maps would be particularly useful here to draw whole areas together in a structured way. Look at past questions and either make detailed plans for an answer or write out the answer in 43 to 45 minutes.

Work intensively for several short periods separated by brief breaks. This maximises the operation of what psychologists call primary and recency effects, where we tend to remember best the beginnings and ends of activities.

Surviving 'exam nerves'

A bit of adrenalin is no bad thing in exams, as it can sharpen concentration. Being so nervous that you cannot see or think straight is of no value at all. There are ways that you can help yourself feel calm on the day.

Relaxation

There are several good books readily available to teach you how to relax e.g. Jane Madders, *Stress and Relaxation*). It is worth practicing relaxation several weeks (or months) before the exams, so that it becomes a habit.

Breathing

Deep slow breaths affect the body, and can make it feel calm when distressed. Take a few deep breaths before going into the exam, and do so again when you are at your place. The very act of stopping, thinking about your breathing, and allowing your body to relax, can help to prevent you making silly mistakes through panicking.

Sleep and exercise

The exam season is a stressful time. Regular exercise will help you survive , and also help you sleep. Don't burn the 'midnight candle' too much; it is usually counterproductive.

Sociology examination check list

Keep the following points in mind during the exam:

1 Read the whole paper through carefully.
2 Select your questions making sure you follow the rubric on the paper.
3 Spend *equal* time on each question, which means about 43 to 44 minutes each, after reading through the paper.
4 Underline key words on the question. Do *not* copy it out onto the answer sheet.
5 Make a brief plan.

The Examination

6 Check that your plan answers the question.
7 Start your essay from a point related to a key issue in the question.
8 Link your essay paragraph by paragraph. Also link the main points regularly back to the question.
9 Back up any arguments with relevant examples.
10 Put in dates where appropriate, e.g. for certain studies, or acts of parliament, etc.
11 Put events in historical sequence if this aids clarity.
12 If you think you are running out of things to say, check if there is another 'angle':

Theory or perspectives	Race
Methods and values	Gender
Objectivity and subjectivity	Education
Stratification	Family
Social mobility	Generation

13 If you run out of time, complete the last question giving the points you would have covered, in 'telegraphic form'.